Guess v

Karolina Kowalska

Guess what...? © 2023 Karolina Kowalska

All rights reserved.

No part of this publication may be reproduced, stored in a retrieval system, or transmitted, in any form or by any means, electronic, mechanical, photocopying, recording or otherwise, without the prior written permission of the presenters.

Karolina Kowalska asserts the moral right to be identified as author of this work.

Presentation by *BookLeaf Publishing*

Web: www.bookleafpub.com

E-mail: info@bookleafpub.com

ISBN: 9789357441346

First edition 2023

DEDICATION

Dreamers and thinkers, this one is for you. What you're dreaming of, you can achieve. This is my dream come true.

ACKNOWLEDGEMENT

Thank you to my parents who always encouraged me to read.

My sister who was a never ending inspiration since our childhood, the main character of my childhood stories and diaries. I hope you know how much of an impact on this you've had.

My nieces who inspire me to notice the tiny moments in life with so much joy and happiness.

Lili, thank you for being my first editor.

Bella, thank you for your making writing poems look easy.

My friends who are always supportive of my crazy ideas (you know who you are!) and I hope this will surprise you, again.

All my mentors who inspired me to take action and make this dream of mine a reality.

I am forever grateful.

PREFACE

These poems were written laughing and crying; at home, in a coffee shop, on the plane, on the beach in Crete, a random bench in the UK parks and shopping malls in Poland as I often wander arounds thinking to myself "guess what...?".
I am grateful for the inspiration hitting me during the best and the worst times and I wanted to share it with you.

Life

In the middle of the night
the storm woke me up
lying there
listening to the loud thunder
tearing the sky
my heartbeat stroke
and then
silence
calm
peace
just like in life.

Stillness

Stillness
That's when you hear nothing
Silence
Breathe in, breathe out
And suddenly
it's there
birds singing
household noise
the fridge
the heating coming on
cat breathing
car passing by outside
all the noises
you can only hear
in stillness

Waking up

I love waking up on a sunny day
to the rays of sunshine lighting up the room
I love waking up to the smell of coffee
I love waking up in freshly washed sheets
I love waking up hearing the cat meowing
I love waking up in the arms of my loved one
I love waking up happy
I love waking up with a song playing in my head
I love waking up feeling grateful
.
.
.

I love waking up.

Gate

All those
moments
of pain, fear
and uncertainty
are the gate
to a beautiful life.
Be brave to open it
and cross to the other side.

Miracle

Take a break
to appreciate
this moment
You
in all your
beauty and scars
Tiny miracle
in the world.

Choose

Choose you
Choose your time
Choose your pleasure
Choose your people
Choose your thoughts
Choose your happiness
Choose your sorrow
Always choose
You.

When

When do your eyes sparkle with joy?
When does your soul want to sing?
When does your heart skip a beat?
When do you laugh so much your belly hurts?
When do you feet want to dance?
Take a note in all those moments
Stop and breathe
Those moments
They are your Happy.

Sugar

Just like sugar
can sweeten up sour flavours
You, my sweet one,
can make your life
deliciously sweet...
Sprinkle some sugar
everywhere you go
and in everything you do
and watch your life transform.

She

She's the moon in the dark sky
She's the sun on a rainy day
She's the sky full of twinkling stars
She's the rain on a dry day
She's the rainbow after the storm
She's the colourful sunset
She's the magical sunrise
She's you

Home

In your eyes
I saw
my now
my future
my forever

In your eyes
I saw
all the moments
I prayed for

In your eyes
I saw
my world

In your eyes
I saw
home

Journey

Go to the place where you belong
Go to the people who love you
Go to the ones that ignite the spark within you
Go to places you feel alive
Go where you feel at peace
Go to those who lift you up
Walk away from anything than that

Brave

Be brave to dream
your wildest dreams

Be brave to follow
your heart's desires

Be brave to sing
your soul's longing

Be brave to know
it's all within you

Be brave enough
to make them happen

River

Your best life
Is yours to live

It's yours to love
It's yours to enjoy

It's yours to swim through
Like a river to the ocean

With ebbs and flows
To finally get
To where it belongs
To meet the destiny

Life lessons

Lessons in life
Don't need to hurt
Don't need to be hard on you
Don't need to be painful

Some lessons you learn
Being your happiest self
Living the best moments
With best people by your side

Remember at school?
Some lessons
You were excited about
And learnt them with joy

Those lessons teach you too!
Cherish them

Tears

Tears
express so much,
shared at the happiest
and the saddest of times.
Tears of joy, fear, shame, guilt,
love, pride, passion, happiness,
deepest and darkest moments,
in moments of pain and relief,
in joy and in grief,
alone and with others.
They mean so much.
I ask you one thing:
Let. Them. Flow.

Beginning

This is not the end,
my darling.

This...
this new path
you are on
is the new beginning.

Start walking
with your head held high
smile on your face
and sunshine in your heart.

Start walking
towards your best life.

Your dreams
will meet you there.

Too many times

Too many times
I said yes
where all I wanted
is to scream no.

Too many times
the tears
were burning my face.

Too many times
my heart broke
longing for something
we weren't.

That one time
I said
no to my tears,
yes to me
and I listened
to my broken heart.

In that moment
I started to be me again.

In that moment
I started to live.

My love

You,
of all the people, you.

You,
of all the places, you.

You,
of all the faces, you.

You,
of all the feelings, you.

It's always been you
and it always will.

My love.

Blank pages

Each day
you wake up
and have a choice
to fill the blank page
of a new day
with the most
beautiful colours

Above the clouds

Above the clouds
the sky is blue

Above the clouds
there is no rain

Above the clouds
the sun shines bright

Above the clouds
I saw the rainbow

Above the clouds
everything's clear

Above the clouds
my mind is still

Above the clouds
I found me

Above the clouds
I set myself free

Voice

I gave my fears voice
I gave my doubts voice
I gave my insecurities voice

The voice so strong
It made me all those things

I crumbled

I searched for a new voice

Slowly
Day by day

I gave forgiveness voice
I gave compassion voice
I gave kindness voice
I gave gratitude voice
I gave self love voice

The voice so strong
The whole new me
Was born

Ingram Content Group UK Ltd.
Milton Keynes UK
UKHW021418040723
424531UK00015B/671